GET HIRED!

RECESSION-PROOF

STRATEGIES FOR FINDING A JOB NOW

SYLVIA ARTHUR

CONTENTS

1. STRATEGY IS EVERYTHING!

THIS BOOK WON'T show you how to write a killer CV. Nor will it tell you how to deliver a job-winning interview. There are thousands of articles, books and websites that will show you how to do all these things and more, but this isn't one of them.

The reason for this is simple. There's no point being the owner of the aforementioned killer CV or possessing award-winning interview skills if there are no jobs for which to apply these essential abilities. That's the story of our time - that there are not enough jobs for those who want them, thanks to the pitiful state of our national and global economies.

But, despite what the media tell us, and what we sometimes take comfort in telling ourselves, there are jobs out there. In fact, there are many. You just have to know where to find them. So this is a book about that. It's about busting the myth that there are no jobs out there by showing you, in practical ways, how and where to find them.

I wrote *Get Hired!* because I wanted to share everything I've learnt over the last five years about finding a job during the worst recession since the Great Depression. Nearly six million people under the age of 25 are currently out of work in Europe. In some countries, more than half of young people wanting to work are unemployed. Employers, HR and recruitment experts and even politicians constantly tell us that a huge gulf exists between the skills that employers require, and those that job seekers possess. Most of the time, this so-called skills gap is blamed on the education system, which is accused of churning out millions of clueless, entitled graduates without a work ethic between them.

Whatever the case, creative approaches to finding jobs need to be employed in the current supply-saturated labour market. The traditional routes of looking for work - newspaper job sections, high-street recruitment agencies, the job centre, and even the comparatively recent phenomenon of online jobs boards - have been made redundant by the severity of the economic crisis and the evolution of the labour market. I've seen and experienced the impact of these twin drivers both as an insider and as an outsider, as a consultant to the European Commission on communicating job mobility and as a job seeker myself. What I've learnt is that the rules of the job search game have changed and, because of this, the mindset of the player must change, too, otherwise you lose.

Thinking strategically, acting strategically

Things have changed dramatically since I was a graduate. When I left university in the late 1990s, eager to enter the world of Fleet Street journalism, looking for a job was simple.

For an aspiring journalist at that time, the thing to do was to buy *The Guardian* newspaper every Monday and Saturday and scour the pages of the reassuringly thick *Media Guardian* supplement. Inside were dozens of adverts from media organisations, large and small, looking to hire reporters, editors, researchers, assistant producers, and every other kind of journalism-related job. Although it was a highly competitive profession to enter, back then, it was to all intents and purposes a job seekers' market.

Today, the *Media Guardian* is a flimsy shadow of its former self. And it's not just aspiring or, even, seasoned journalists who are struggling to find work in these straitened times; everyone is. It's not that the old ways don't work; they just need to be adapted. By all means, pick up a newspaper to look for a job; just don't expect to find it in the classifieds section.

And, if you do, be prepared for fierce competition. On average, every corporate job opening attracts 250 applications, but only four to six of these applicants will be called for an interview, and only one of those will be offered a job[i].

This is only one such figure of gloom. The statistics as a whole tell a worrying tale about the prospects for finding work today. It's a virtual lottery. As a recent History graduate lamented to me, looking for a job now is "a hustle."

Perhaps it's always been that way, but there's been something of a power shift in the last decade or so. The old adage, "It's not what you know but who you know" still holds true, but the deeply entrenched elitism that made certain jobs the exclusive domain of the chosen few has been somewhat turned on its head.

Technology has proved to be a great leveller. Professional networking sites like LinkedIn™, and real world Meetup™ events, have made it easier than ever to connect with those with hiring power in formal and informal ways, lessening the barriers that previously existed, even if they haven't been completely eroded.

But because the demand for jobs far outstrips the supply, the onus is now on job seekers to distinguish themselves from the crowd and to carve out their own paths. Job seekers need to be smart. They need to approach the job search from all angles making sure to cover all bases. To do this, they need to think differently, and act differently, too. In short, they need to get strategic, fast.

The 360° thinker

What, exactly, does this mean? It means committing to an approach to job seeking that is proactive and based on evidence rather than hope. It requires research and analysis, and empathy, too, by assuming the role of a recruiter and placing yourself inside the mind of an employer. The 360° Job Search™, as its name implies, is a comprehensive approach to job seeking that allows you to make the most of the information and resources available to uncover the myriad opportunities they present. It means developing a whole new way of thinking and doing.

It's not so much about thinking outside the box as smashing it wide open. Everything you know about looking for a job is useful, but it's no longer enough. If you're serious about looking for a job, then you also need to be serious about *finding* a job. The key is in the latter verb. *To find* is different from *to look* and indicates success in the act of searching. Being strategic is about looking *and* finding. Hard work and dedication are necessary. Being strategic isn't just a frame of mind; it's also a way of life. Perhaps the following figures and a brief anecdote will illustrate the necessity for adopting a new strategy.

Indeed.com, the world's most popular jobs site, boasts more than 150 million unique visitors every month and operates in 55 countries, [ii] probably yours. One of its main competitors, Monster.com, says that, every minute on its worldwide network, 29 CVs are uploaded, 7,900 jobs are searched and 2,800 jobs are viewed[iii]. That's a lot of competition for seemingly few jobs.

But when you add to this the fact that up to 80% of job vacancies are never actually advertised, it begins to dawn on you that you really are screwed. You start to realise just how narrow and unrealistic your current job search strategy is, that is, if you even have one, if you rely in whole or in part on online job boards and advertising as your main source of leads.

The last place I would go to find a job on the Internet is a mega online job board. Neither would top recruiters. "In the H.R. world, applicants from Monster or other job boards carry a stigma," says one such hirer, who disparagingly refers to the site as "Monster.ugly." [iv] That's not to suggest avoiding job boards altogether. These sites are useful for finding other vital information about the labour market and recruitment trends, which I'll elaborate on later.

The 360° equation

Let's start with some maths: 25% of the workforce is actively looking for a job. That's a quarter of the working population who are aggressively pursuing the 20%, or one-fifth of jobs that are advertised. If you rely on traditional job search methods, that's already a 5% deficit working against you in the surplus of demand in relation to supply.

On the flipside, the 75% of the workforce that is passive (i.e., that isn't actively looking for a job) is, by its nature, the most sought-after group. Since passive candidates are generally satisfied in their jobs, they tend to be good performers and respected by their peers. Those in this category are in the enviable position of having a 5% advantage. The 80%, or four-fifths of jobs that are unadvertised are theirs for the offering as recruiters go all out to entice them from their current employer. Comparatively, there's much more room for manoeuvre in this passive space.

The statistics are even more favourable for the passive group when you deduct the 15% of workers who are deemed to be 'on the cusp,' that is, open to finding a new job but not yet actively looking. That leaves 60% of passive candidates in an 80% pool, a clear inversion of the demand-supply ratio.

Passive candidates have options. If they choose, they could come swimming in your 20% pool, drowning you out even further. The problem is you don't have the chance to do the same; you're confined to the overcrowded 25/20 shallow end because you don't have a pass to the deep end.

The LinkedIn 2015 *Global Recruiting Trends* report revealed that 26% of employers plan to source passive candidates in the next twelve months. That's just over a quarter of employers who won't be looking for you if you don't get smart and distinguish yourself from the crowd.

That's why you need a strategy.

The 360° approach

I know about this hidden job market from personal experience. When I worked at a communications agency in Brussels in 2010, one of my tasks was to sift through the hundreds of CVs the company would receive. Some of these were unsolicited, applications sent in on the off chance that there might be an opening, but many were in response to ads the company would place on various online job boards.

Two things never failed to amaze me when I engaged in this long, laborious and often torturous process. The first was the sheer number of applications we would receive for just one post. Anything between 200 and 300 CVs was the norm and not just from job seekers based in Brussels, or Belgium, even, but from all over Europe and the world. Secondly, I was always shocked at the generic nature of the applications. It was clear that the majority of applicants hadn't even bothered to tailor their CV and cover letter to the post let alone read the job description.

In the end, these posts were usually filled by people who hadn't even applied for them, either through referrals or by headhunting / poaching, but more on that later. The point of this story is that you can no longer afford to do what you've always done when it comes to looking for work. You need a new methodology for uncovering and tapping into that 80% of jobs, the vast majority, that are unadvertised and, as such, aren't being pursued by the masses who frequent Indeed.com and its like.

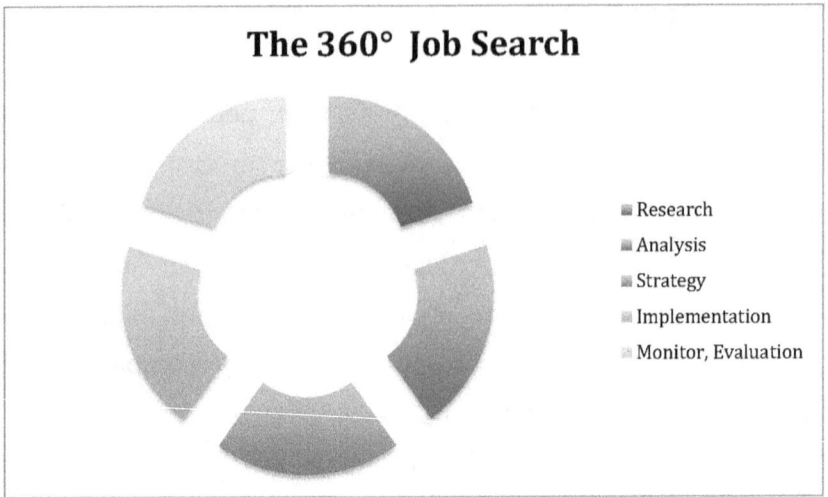

The 360° Job Search

- Research
- Analysis
- Strategy
- Implementation
- Monitor, Evaluation

This is what the 360° job search methodology does. It brings together the various elements of the new job search into a straightforward system that comprises of the following building blocks:

- **Research**

  Actively and passively collecting data from a broad range of sources including print, broadcast and online media, government agencies, recruitment agencies, local, national and international sources and more. See below.

- **Analysis**

  Dissecting and analysing the collected data to better understand it in order to make informed decisions on the basis of hard facts and evidence. What does this data mean for me? What should I do with it? How should I apply it?

- **Strategy**

  Developing and drafting a written job search strategy, with SMART objectives, integrating each of the 360° elements.

- **Implementation**

  Creating a structured, practical action plan with daily, weekly and monthly actions and goals to implement the strategy and achieve its stated objectives.

- **Monitoring and Evaluation**

  Regular monitoring of strategy and action plan progress in order to take stock of achievements and know whether to tweak, change or abandon actions.

A word about research

Research, the seeking out and collection of information or data, is the bedrock of the 360° approach. Without information, and inside information at that, finding a job in the current climate is practically impossible.

The research phase of the 360° job search relies on two types of data collection: active and passive.

Active data collection is the aggressive pursuit of information from a range of sources using an assortment of methods, channels and tools, some of which are outlined in the following chapters.

Passive data collection requires less work in that the

information comes to you rather than you having to seek it out but its analysis is of equal importance and deserves the same attention as active research. Passive data collection comes in the form of newsletters sent directly to your inbox, press releases, alerts and other such messages.

At the beginning of your 360° job search, you should be doing 80% active research, 20% passive. In actuality, active data collection requires 100% of your efforts at the start of your journey, but I say 80% because you may already be receiving sources of jobs information that you don't yet recognise as such.

As time goes on, active data collection will gradually decrease until half, if not most, of the information you receive is passive, leaving more time for analysis and the relative fun of the implementation phase (i.e. networking and social media engagement).

Some job seekers prefer to set up an email address specifically for receiving passive data so that this information collection is separate from their personal emails. Do this if you choose, but make sure to check your account regularly to avoid missing out on important, time-sensitive information.

The new hustle: get smart to get hired

Being strategic isn't just about setting goals. It's about having a plan to achieve those goals. Moreover, it's about that plan being different from, and more effective than, everyone else's. An athlete wouldn't run a race with the same game plan as her opponent and neither should you. Today's job market is more competitive than ever so the savvy job seeker knows to adapt his or her approach in order to get away from the pack, and get ahead.

What is the Strategic Hustle?

- It's more of the strategy and less of the hustle.
- It's an investment, with short, medium and long-term dividends.
- It's the smart way of finding jobs while others are looking.
- It's meritocratic: it's about what you know as much as who you know.
- It works!

Searching for a job now requires a level of planning and innovation previously unneeded. This book is a collection of the most effective methods, strategies and tools that I've discovered for finding a job now. The strategies work for any country and in any economy.

In this book, I make a number of assumptions. The first is that you know or have a strong idea about the industry or sector you want to work in. I also assume a degree of flexibility in your thinking, in terms of both industry and sector, and geographic location. Organisations are multinational and so are opportunities. The more adaptable you are in terms of where you're prepared to live and work, the more abundant your opportunities will be.

Chapter 2 shows you how to read with your eyes wide

open, listen with your ears tuned into the right frequency and consume media intelligently to find the jobs that are hidden behind the headlines and between the waves.

Chapter 3 explains how to use data from government agencies to get the heads-up on businesses expanding in your chosen area, and the opportunities that these new openings and investments provide.

Chapter 4 is all about getting aggressive with your network and actively engaging with your contacts to get the inside scoop on internal openings so that you put yourself in prime position to be passively recruited.

Chapter 5 asks you to place yourself inside the mind of a recruiter. It unearths a goldmine of information that will enable you to acquire the intelligence on recruitment trends that, when applied, will set you apart from the competition.

Chapter 6 will help you take your job search international by making the most of your local public employment service to source information on foreign labour markets and help you make informed decisions.

Each of these chapters embeds the first two stages of the 360° approach, research and evaluation, and ends with a list of actions you can take to start building your strategy.

Chapter 7 brings all this information together and shows you how to take what you've learnt and develop a strategy and action plan that will guide you in achieving your professional goals.

The final section, the appendix, lists various websites, resources, templates and tools that you can use now and in the future to take control of your career and chart its progress.

Today, everyone should be a career strategist. The economic crisis won't last forever, but it makes sense to arm yourself against the ups and downs of the labour market.

The strategies in this book for finding a job are timeless. By putting into practice the advice laid out here, you will improve your chances of securing work. I did. I didn't always get the job, or even an interview, but I did find opportunities and, in the process, make essential contacts that I can use down the line. You can, too.

And when you do, don't forget to let us know how you got hired by employing the recession-proof strategies you discovered in this book.

But, before then, there's work to do.

Now, let's get strategic. Let's get hired!

The 360° Manifesto

- I will be methodical
- I will be analytical
- I will love data
- I will be organised
- I will be proactive
- I will swim against the tide
- I will be inquisitive and have an open mind
- I will be in the right place at the right time
- I will persevere
- I will get hired!

2. READ BETWEEN THE LINES

I ALWAYS LOOK forward to receiving my copy of *PR Week* in the mail. As a communications professional, the weekly newsmagazine is compulsory reading for keeping up-to-date with the latest happenings in the public relations industry. It's an essential piece of any communicator's kit, like a tablet or a smartphone.

One evening in January 2013, while reading the magazine from cover to cover, I came across a story that made me sit up and take notice:

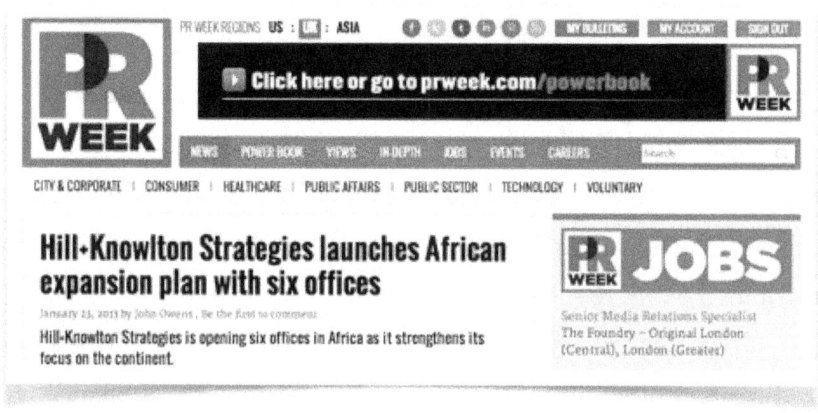

Hill+Knowlton launches African expansion plan[v]

For those who don't know, Hill+Knowlton Strategies is a subsidiary of WPP, one of the world's largest advertising and communications agencies. H+K, itself, is a multinational firm, employing thousands of staff in offices in most major markets.

The decision to expand across Africa was exciting news, for H+K and for me. I had been thinking about changing jobs for a while and I saw the opening of six new bases in Africa as an opportunity for an ambitious comms professional to be in at the start of a crucial phase in the organisation's growth. I had also been considering making the move to another country, and not just to another job, and South Africa had been in my mind as a vibrant place to live and work.

I acted fast. I set about tracking down the CEO of H+K Africa, who was mentioned in the article. I wanted to be among the first to express my interest in this attractive and, no doubt, competitive opportunity and I wanted to make it clear that I would be willing to relocate.

I Googled his name and, although I was unable to find his email address in this initial simple search, it was valuable for discovering other useful information. I was able to glean data on his professional background and his interests, and review his current work by reading recent editions of the company newsletter in which he'd penned the editorials. I would use all this when crafting an email to introduce myself to him.

Needless to say, I did eventually find his email address and I did contact him within 48 hours of the piece being published. I'll explain more about the outcome of this strategy later, and how it put me in prime position for a prestigious job that hadn't even been advertised.

The point I want to make is that jobs like this are all over the media – in the news pages, in the business section, in the people profiles, everywhere. You just have to be open to recognising them.

How to read, listen and watch 'the news'

It's not just the trade press that's brimming with news that could bolster your job search. The mainstream media - newspapers, magazines, television and radio news, and websites – is overflowing with job leads like the H+K one. You just need to be able to spot them by adjusting the way you consume and interpret the news.

In November 2014, I was listening to the *Today* programme on BBC Radio 4 as I did every morning. My six a.m. alarm had not long gone off and I was snoozing, letting the show play on as my soundtrack in the background.

At the time, I was living in Barcelona, Spain. I tuned in to the show from my iPhone through an app called TuneIn *Radio* that allows users to stream live radio broadcasts from stations around the world.

About an hour through the programme, a business item came on that caught my attention. It was about the British entrepreneur, Sir James Dyson, he of the bagless vacuum fame and countless other engineering innovations. Prior to the segment, the journalist trailed the feature on a couple of occasions, teasing listeners that the Dyson CEO would be making a big announcement during the course of the interview.

News about Dyson always interested me. Sir James had been a vocal critic of the lack of trained engineers being produced in the UK and he had long spoken of his need to recruit engineers from abroad to fill his open vacancies.

When the interview aired around seven-thirty, it was full of interesting information. Dyson announced that the company would be creating 3000 jobs by 2020 in the biggest expansion in its history, which would cost upwards of £200 million. Were I an engineer or a scientist, I thought, I'd be racing to send in my application.

As well as featuring on the *Today* programme, the item on Sir James Dyson and his pledge to create 3000 new engineering jobs featured on the BBC Breakfast News television show and the BBC website. A quick search of Google News showed that most of the major print newspapers and their websites also covered the story, including the *Financial Times, The Guardian* and *The Telegraph*.

If you're an engineer actively or passively looking for work, there's no reason why you shouldn't have:

a) Heard of these opportunities and, after listening to the *Today* programme, or reading about the expansion in the press or on the Internet;

b) Pounced on these opportunities.

Whether you're based in Leatherhead, Leipzig or Lodz, if you're looking for work and you can access the Internet, then you have everything you need to find a job now. All it takes is better reading, improved listening and the application of an analytical mind. The following sections will show you how to develop all three.

Deconstructing a 'news' story for hidden jobs

This is not a news story. It's a job advert dressed up as a news story. It's an invitation to submit an application for a post that's yet to be advertised, or may never be advertised. Read it as you normally would, then read it very carefully, paying close attention to the highlighted sections:

Hill+Knowlton launches African expansion plan

January 23, 2013 by John Owens

Hill+Knowlton Strategies is opening six offices in Africa as it strengthens its focus on the continent.

The strategy includes the launch of new bases in Uganda, Tanzania, Rwanda and Ghana — and the near-term formation of offices in Nigeria and South Africa.

Jack Martin, global chairman and CEO of Hill+Knowlton Strategies, said: 'The pan-African strategy culminates years of successful research by H+K in emerging markets, particularly in Africa, where we see the potential for exponential growth for current and prospective clients.

'Investing in Africa is a key pillar of H+K's global strategy, as we are committed to the continent's tremendous development

---

potential and diverse cultures across the region.'

The move comes after Edelman shifted its global structuring to take in growth within Asia and Africa.

'Our strategy recognises that sustained growth of businesses, local or multinational, can best be supported by experienced, homegrown talent with a pan-African perspective' said Alexander Döll, the first CEO of H+K Strategies Africa, who previously led H+K's East Africa operation.

'This plan ensures we have the local knowledge and experience needed to expand that world-class service across the continent.'

H+K Strategies entered the sub-Saharan Africa region in May 2009 through a joint venture with Scangroup, a Kenya-based marketing and comms firm listed on the Nairobi Securities Exchange (NSE), with an office opening in Nairobi.

The outfit has supported global, multinational and local brands, including Procter & Gamble, Nokia, Coca-Cola, Airtel, Nestlé, Emirates, Standard Chartered, Sony, De La Rue and DHL.

Source: PR Week

These are the highlights I made in the print issue of *PR Week* on the story about H+K Strategies Africa expansion plans. It's a thorough deconstruction of the piece, complete with severe underlining and margin notes.

What follows is an explanation of the analysis in order to uncover the real story behind the story and reveal the hidden job/s. Here's the breakdown:

Paragraph / Sentence	Comment
1 / -	The story. Context.
2 / -	I was open to working in any one of the six new bases that were being established and I stressed this in my email to the African CEO while also mentioning my preference for South Africa and Ghana.
3 / -	It was unlikely that I'd get an audience with the global chairman and CEO so it was never in my plans to contact him. However, it was good to know his name so I could research who he was, what he had done for the company and where he planned to take it. All this would feed into my email and later interaction with the CEO of H+K Strategies Africa, mentioned below.
4 / -	Investigate. Download.
5 / -	Edelman is a competitor of H+K and it was an interesting bit of information to know that they too were shifting their

	focus to Africa. I could reference this in future correspondence.
6 / 1	Although I wasn't "homegrown talent," I was experienced and had the pan-African perspective the company was looking for.
6 / 2	The man to contact. Research. Check LinkedIn. Do I have any 1st, 2nd or 3rd connections?
6 / 3	Look into what he did at H+K East Africa.
8 / 1	What have they done since 2009? Any achievements of note?
8 / 2	Look into. Research.
9 / 1	Find out what work they've done with these brands and reference in email.

Any news story with even a hint of a lead can and should be deconstructed like this. When reading a news article in any media, be judicious and look out for this significant information embedded within the text:

- **Names**
  Representatives from the organisation who've been quoted and / or referred to.
- **Numbers**
  Facts, figures, and key dates.
- **News**
  It is, ostensibly, a news piece after all. But, go

behind the headlines to work out: What's the story? What's the issue at stake? Why is it important? How can I help solve the problem? This will give you much-needed context when reaching out to named contacts.

When you come across a story with potential, save it. Clip it using Evernote or print a copy and keep it in a cuttings folder. Then begin your research again by finding out more about the company, the global context and the individuals named. Be well organised and be prepared to act on your stash of clippings. Set yourself deadlines with reminders for following up because jobs, like news, have an expiry date. What's here today is gone tomorrow. There's nothing worse than being blessed with opportunity and failing to seize it because you were too slow to act. So get going.

360° awareness: levels of engagement

So now you know *how* to read, listen and watch the media to tease out job leads, the obvious follow-up question is: *What* should I read, listen to and watch? *Where* should I go for news with job potential?

The first thing to be aware of is that news comes from a variety of sources at a variety of levels. You need to be on top of them all. There's international, pan-European and national press as well as regional and local media. Furthermore, there's the trade or specialist press dedicated to a particular industry or sector. *PR*

Week, for instance, is aimed at public relations specialists but there's also *Marketing Week* and *Advertising Age* for marketers and media professionals more generally.

Many media in these categories are accessible on the Internet and many are free, but some, like *The Financial Times,* impose a paywall after a certain number of visits. But, if you know what you're looking for, you can often get around this restriction by searching for the headline in Google News and accessing it from there rather than direct from the news site itself. You could also try loading the page through a private browsing or Incognito window.

Segmenting the media into various streams and engaging with them all is an integral element of the 360° job search. You may be wondering why you should bother with the international press when you're looking for a job in your local area. The answer is simple: business is multinational and so is news.

An announcement from a major US corporation that it will create 500 jobs in some small corner of Europe will certainly make headlines in the US. It will probably gain traction in the European media, and there's even more chance that it will feature in the national press in the country in which the organisation is expanding.

But, perhaps it won't, and that's why it pays to have all bases covered. Even if it does, it will be good to get the news from different perspectives and mine the contacts that will be named and quoted in the write-ups.

The figure below illustrates the various media levels that you should regularly engage with. Remember, the purpose of this

360° approach to media consumption is twofold: to find job leads that you can actively pursue and to keep you on top of what's happening in the international and national labour markets:

'Press and media' encompasses print, broadcast and online media in various formats:

Print	Broadcast	Online
Newspapers (Free and paid for, quality broadsheets)	Television (News, business programming)	Websites (News, business, trade, industry and sector specific)
Magazines (General, trade and specialist)	Radio (News, business programming)	Blogs (Industry and sector specific)

Reports, studies (General and industry / sector specific)		Podcasts (General and industry and sector specific)
		Apps
		YouTube
		Newsletters

Your basic media toolkit

There are staples that you should have in your 360° toolkit, regardless of your profession. Some will be the source of job leads while others will increase your general labour market knowledge and keep you abreast of industry news.

The following is a recommended media list that incorporates media from the range of levels:

Newspapers (online or print)
- The Financial Times (International / Europe / UK)
- The Wall Street Journal (International / Europe)
- The Daily Telegraph (National)
- The Guardian (National)
- International Business Times UK (International / National)

Newsmagazines (online or print)
- The Economist (International / Europe)
- Inc. (International)

- Fortune (International)
- Wired (UK)
- European CEO (Europe)
- Management Today (National)

Television (live)

- BBC Breakfast (BBC1) (National)
- Channel 4 News (Channel 4) (National)
- Sky News paper review (Sky News) (National)
- Newsnight (BBC2) (National)

Radio (live or podcast)

- Today programme (BBC Radio 4) (National)
- In Business (BBC Radio 4) (National)
- The Bottom Line (BBC Radio 4) (National)

Websites

- BBC News (Online)
- LinkedIn Pulse (Online)

This is by no means an exhaustive list and you should customise it with your own regional and local media, but it's enough to get you started, whatever type of job you're looking for. By all means add to it and expand it. Adapt it to the country or countries you're interested in working in. Consume the suggested media in whichever way works for you, print, broadcast or online, live or on replay, on any device of your choosing.

The key is to incorporate these tactics into your daily life until you don't even realise what you're doing; you're just doing it - intelligently consuming news with a purpose and a payoff.

Completing the circle: putting your research into action

When you open a newspaper or listen to a news programme or read a news story online, read it as if you're reading a job advert. Whether it's the announcement of a company expansion or an employer decrying a lack of skills that are impeding his company's growth, the story should be interpreted as someone crying out for the right person to get in contact and solve his / her problem.

It doesn't take much to find out the email address or telephone number of a company representative mentioned in an article. A simple Google search will usually do the trick or, better still a search on LinkedIn will reveal how you're connected to the person you need to get to. The great thing about using LinkedIn is that not only can you be personally introduced by a mutual contact, but it also shows that you're ahead of the game when it comes to making the most of your network. In essence, it shows that you're serious about both your job search and your career.

In conclusion to my story about H+K Strategies, I eventually made my approach to Alexander Döll, the CEO of H+K Strategies Africa, via LinkedIn. After a comprehensive Google search in which I found out not only his work email address, but more about the man and his professional passions, I spent a couple of days carefully crafting an email. In it, I not only made reference to the *PR Week* article in which I had read the original news piece about H+K's Africa expansion plans but, as a result of my research, I could also allude to other things that I knew would pique his interest and show that I had done my homework, that I was a serious potential candidate.

To further consolidate this impression, I took advantage of a LinkedIn offer that had been sitting in my inbox to upgrade to Premium for a free trial period, which would give me access to InMail. InMail allows users to send messages directly to another LinkedIn member that they're not connected to, something you're unable to do with a free account. I could have simply emailed him through his work address but I feared my message would get lost in the flood or wouldn't get past his secretary's screening. So I decided the best way to go was to cut out the middleman and go direct.

My strategy worked. Within 24 hours, I had received a response from the CEO of a branch of one of the world's leading marketing and communications firms. He was impressed by my initiative and was eager to meet me. Fortunately, he would be in the UK on a business trip the following week and, since I would be in London too, we arranged to meet.

The informal interview went well. We discussed business over a Lebanese lunch for almost two hours, including where I was prepared to move and when I could start. Yes, I was offered the job. I had achieved a breakthrough and I fully intended to capitalise on it. You can, too. Just be sure to read the 'news.'

ACTIONS

- Read better. Read closely and read widely.
- Keep your eyes open for news items that are more than news. Read these as if you're reading a job advert. Pull out the relevant information (e.g. jobs available, skills needed, names of contact people etc.) and plan how to act on it.

- Identify the right person to contact. Not everyone mentioned in the article will be appropriate.

- Always use LinkedIn as well as Google to research named contacts in an article.

- Use LinkedIn's InMail function to contact senior people. Take a free trial before committing to Premium.

- Read the quality press. The broadsheets, or their online versions, should be read daily. Sign up to receive their e-newsletters so you have the latest news waiting in your inbox in the morning ready to act on.

- Sign up to receive the newspaper front pages by email at The Paperboy.com. Get an insight into what's on the inside pages by reading The Papers on the BBC news blog.

- Subscribe to industry magazines. Whether you're an architect, an engineer or a caterer, there's a publication for every profession. If you can't afford to subscribe, see if there's a cheaper online-only subscription. Alternatively, ask your local library to subscribe.

- Read quality news websites. Pay particular attention to the business and economy sections. Try getting around the paywall by searching Google News for stories using the headline.

- Listen to quality radio. Download an app like TuneIn Radio that gives you access to live radio broadcasts from around the world. Find out which quality radio programmes air in your country of choice and be sure to tune into them regularly and / or download their podcasts.

- Keep a cuttings file. This can be virtual, using a tool like Evernote or hardcopy clippings from newspapers and magazines.

3. FYI: FDI

GOVERNMENTS, LIKE INDIVIDUALS, are hustlers. The difference is that, while you're out there hustling for a job, they're hustling for cash, which more or less amounts to the same thing.

Governments spend millions in an effort to entice foreign companies to invest in their countries by opening new offices, establishing research and development centres and headquartering their regional operations, thereby bringing jobs to their citizens who in turn inject money into the economy.

The battle to attract Foreign Direct Investment, or FDI, is competitive. Governments go head-to-head to outdo each other with incentives like subsidies and tax breaks in order to ensure that inward investment comes to them rather than going elsewhere. FDI includes crossborder corporate expansion, investment promotion and economic development. It's a lucrative business, for organisations and for governments and proves the old adage "you've got to spend money to make money" still holds true.

Interesting though this is, you may be wondering why I'm telling you this. The reason is that Foreign Direct Investment has become the major economic driver of globalisation. Companies are rapidly globalising through FDI to serve new markets and customers, map out their value chains in the most efficient locations globally, and to access technological and natural resources.

According to Ernst & Young's EU Attractiveness Survey for 2014 [vi] , 54% of respondents were optimistic that Europe's attractiveness as an FDI destination will continue to improve in the next three years.

FDI in Europe reached a record high in 2013. The region received €223bn in inward investment, up 25 per cent year on year. The nearly 4,000 FDI projects – up from 3,800 in 2012 – created 166,000 jobs[vii].

That's a job for you if you know where to find it.

Let me show you where.

What is FDI and what can it do for me? The case of Ireland

I remember feeling exhilarated following a meeting in Galway, Ireland in June 2014. My colleague and I had been invited to speak to the Irish national EURES network about the work we had been doing with the Dublin central office. For the past six months, we had been developing a communications strategy for attracting tech professionals from across Europe to Ireland, who were in hot demand by employers nationally.

The meeting went exceptionally well. The advisers were welcoming and open to hearing our suggestions, and they were full of ideas, frustrations and, finally, optimism about a way forward.

Although historically a nation of emigration, Ireland has, in recent years, become a country of immigration, attracting new residents from mainland Europe and around the world. With growth returning to the economy and jobs being created at a northward rate, there were fears that supply could soon outstrip demand. This fear was particularly being felt in the mushrooming tech sector, which has transformed Dublin into Europe's Silicon Valley.

Ireland is brimming with entrepreneurial spirit and opportunity. Optimism in the form of inward investment is high. Nine of the top 10 US ICT companies are operating in Ireland. The country has one of the highest concentrations of ICT activity and employment in the OECD. It also boasts the leading cluster of MedTech industries employing the highest per capita of Medical Technology personnel in Europe. Eight of the top 20 global companies have a manufacturing base in Ireland[viii].

Controversial corporate tax breaks for foreign investors have drawn many of the world's biggest tech companies to the Irish Republic. Microsoft, Apple, Google, Paypal, eBay, Facebook, Twitter, Instagram, LinkedIn and Airbnb all have their European headquarters on the Emerald Isle. This development has created a demand for new workers with a particular kind of profile. Organisations need highly skilled, multilingual, multicultural staff to service their multilingual, multicultural clients.

Because of a shortage of this type of candidate in Ireland, the tech companies joined forces to fund Make IT in Ireland to attract tech professionals from across the EU to the country. Good pay, great living and working conditions and a vibrant, social culture were just a few of the perks of relocation for adventurous techies willing to make the move.

It's not just techies who benefit from a buoyant technology sector. You'd be right to assume that the establishment or expansion of an IT company would create only IT vacancies – software developers, front-end developers, back-end developers, and the like.

But who will cater for these new employees? They've got to eat, right? They'll make a mess at their desks, and their offices will need cleaning. They'll need help with doing basic admin. They may be experts at programming but they're rubbish at real spelling, right? They'll need cleaners and cooks, administrative and support staff, communications and marketing specialists, accountants and lawyers, the list goes on and on.

The respected economist Enrico Moretti, author of *The New Geography of Jobs*, says that when a high-tech company hires one person, five new non-tech jobs are created[ix]. Although so-called innovation jobs are a small minority of total employment, Moretti believes that the reason the European brain hubs of London, Stockholm, Munich and Amsterdam are thriving is that the growth of innovation generates wealth that supports the 65% of workers who are employed in the local service sector. "The best way for a city to generate jobs for less educated workers is to attract high-tech companies that hire highly educated ones," Moretti says.

So now you know why FDI is important for you *and* your government, here's how to get the scoop on major new investments before the masses do.

Where can I source FDI data?

The most bountiful source of information on new company establishments and expansions is the national inward investment promotion agency. It's the agency's job to actively solicit FDI and they're all too keen to shout about it when they do. You can find the website of any national FDI agency through a simple Google search.

In the case of Ireland, it's the IDA that's responsible for attracting investment into the country. Their website is full of stories, statistics and sales pitches about the benefits of doing business in Ireland. There are many ways to connect with the IDA, they have a presence on virtually all social media platforms, and the website invites you to get in touch either in person, by phone or by mail through any one of its numerous international offices.

However, the most useful tool on the IDA website is the Newsroom. This area, which is accessible to everyone and not just members of the media, hosts press releases, featured articles, blog posts and publications chock full of potential job leads. Even better, you can also sign up to receive the IDA newsletter and ask to be put on the press release list.

Give yourself as many opportunities as possible to find and receive information. I get, on average, four to twelve emails a month from the IDA announcing new FDI projects and its resultant job creation. FDI news may not always make it into the press, but it will make it into your inbox if you sign up to receive updates. And in case you miss the mail in the deluge that is your inbox, follow the IDA on LinkedIn for the news to appear on your homepage timeline.

Organise the information you receive. I started collating the IDA press alerts into a spreadsheet. The purpose of this was to collect in one place all new leads for potential consultancy work, extracting only the key information and tracking my interaction with each new contact, from initial email to meetings to follow-up. Here's a sample from the first quarter of 2014:

Company and website	Press release title and link	Press release summary (inc. date, no. of new jobs over no. years; location)	Business sector	Named contact(s)	Recruitment link (if applicable)
Viagogo Group www.viagogo.com	viagogo Group establishes New Operations Centre in Limerick, Ireland	**Wednesday 2nd July 2014** · The viagogo Group, which operates viagogo.com, the world's largest ticket marketplace, is to open a purpose built international operations centre in Limerick, Ireland. The Limerick operations centre is recruiting for a wide variety of technical and customer service roles for people with a range of skills and languages. Besides English, the centre is presently hiring German, French, Italian, and Spanish speakers as well.	viagogo Group, which operates viagogo.com, is the world's largest ticket exchange, offering its service to customers in around 100 countries.	Edward Parkinson, Operations Manager for the viagogo Group	http://www.jobs.ie/ApplyForJob.aspx?Id=13
NuVasive www.nuvasive.com	NuVasive®, Inc. establishes its International Operation Centre in Waterford	**Monday, 30th June 2014** · NuVasive, Inc. has established an **International Operations Centre in Waterford,** with the creation of up to 30 **highly skilled roles over the next two to three years.** NuVasive has begun hiring **supply chain, customer service, accounting, and IT positions.**	Medical device company	Alex Lukianov, Chairman and CEO Michael Dendinger, Director, NuVasive Ireland Margie Elsesser Corporate Communications	N/A
AdRoll www.adroll.com	AdRoll Doubles Dublin Office Space and Announces 100 Extra Jobs	**26 June 2014** · AdRoll, the world's most widely adopted retargeting platform, **launched new offices in Dublin today** and **announced plans to expand its European operations by doubling its office space and hiring 100 additional staff**	AdRoll is the global leader in retargeting, with over 15,000 active advertisers worldwide. The company's innovative and easy-to-use marketing platform enables brands of all sizes to create personalized ad campaigns based on their own website data, ensuring maximum return on online advertising spend. With a 97 percent customer retention rate, AdRoll provides unmatched transparency and reach across the largest display inventory sources, including Google AdX, Twitter, and Facebook.	Aaron Bell, AdRoll CEO	N/A

Another, overlooked outlet for FDI news is the humble in-flight magazine. I spend a lot of time on planes and reading through the airline's magazine has become more than a way to pass the time between departure and arrival. It's essential material for investment news and job leads. Read them forensically. If you don't fly like other people take busses, you can always view the latest issue of an airline's magazine on issuu.com. Alternatively, download it from the publisher's website or find it by Googling the airline name plus "inflight magazine."

Finally, it's not only those who are looking for work abroad who should mine FDI data for leads. The smart, strategic 360° job seeker knows that s/he can mine gold wherever they dig for data.

Even if you don't want to move, you can still benefit from the freely available data that your national, regional or local development agencies provide. Sign up to receive press releases, newsletters and other updates and be sure to act on them fast. Look out for information on companies that are exporting as a sign of internal expansion and potential job leads. Take advantage of the fact that you're already based in or near the investment area to do a fact-finding mission. Go out and meet people in the know. Expand your network and it may just help you secure a prospect closer to home.

You can also search the database of companies that

have been awarded government contracts and contact them directly. This is publicly available information that can be found on the UK government's Contract Finder website.

Using FDI agencies as employment agencies

This is a snippet from a press alert I received from IDA Ireland in December 2014:

> 10th December 2014 - Dublin - Leading international health and life insurer, **Allianz Worldwide Care, has announced it is to create 100 new positions in Dublin** and move into a number of newly purchased offices in Park West Business Campus, Dublin 12, where its Irish Branch is currently based. **The new roles will span the entire business with an emphasis on claims, helpline and client services, medical services, underwriting and pricing.**
>
> *My emphasis. Source: IDA Ireland*

Like the news story we dissected in a previous chapter, this press release is easily deconstructed. The same, three-step process we used for analysing the *PR Week* article – Names, Numbers, News – can also be applied here, but press releases usually make it easier to identify key information as opposed to the hidden treasure format of news stories.

Again, this news release reinforces the principle of never dismissing a news item on face value. A quick read of the alert shows that the breadth of opportunities available at this specialised company, in this case, insurance, are varied. Here, new openings created by the company's expansion range from customer services to medical services to underwriting and pricing.

Further on in the full version of this press release, the Chief Executive of Allianz Worldwide Care, Ron Buchan is quoted as saying, "The 100 people coming on board will benefit from long term development and training opportunities, and experience a client-focused culture which has enabled the company to grow steadily, even in times of economic uncertainty." Development, training, growth in times of economic uncertainty... all music to the ears of the 360 job seeker.

The release ends by instructing readers to visit the Allianz website for more information on the new job vacancies or, alternatively, to contact the Allianz Worldwide Care HR team directly. That is what I'd do.

I'd also drop a line to one or both of the two public relations executives, whose contact details are given at the bottom of the release, complete with email addresses and telephone numbers. Cover all bases. Get as much inside intelligence as possible.

There's nothing unique about this Allianz press release and the opportunities it flags. I receive anywhere from four to twelve emails from the IDA each month telling me before anyone else that new companies will soon be opening up bases in Ireland.

This passive data is gratefully received as a source of new contacts and potential new prospects. Anyone can get their hands on this freely available information. You should before they do.

Using FDI to choose your relocation destination

There's another way you could use FDI data to help shape your job search and your long-term career strategy.

European Cities and Regions of the Future is an annual study of the most promising investment locations in Europe. Produced by fDi magazine, a subscription-only, online and print magazine from the *Financial Times*, it publishes an annual ranking of top FDI destinations around the world.

These rankings are aggregated and filtered using a variety of criteria into useful, bite-size nuggets of information. There are charts that rank regions, e.g. top cities in north, south, east and west Europe; economic potential; human capital and lifestyle; top large, mid-sized, small and micro cities, and so on. If you're flexible about where you're willing to work and don't mind relocating, this data is invaluable for helping you make informed decisions about potential locations.

Like press releases, and targeted research and events for employers, which we'll come on to later, this information isn't designed for you. It's compiled for corporate decision-makers and crossborder investment professionals, governments and their agencies, businesses and industries, people who work in and around FDI and members of the press.

But, there's nothing stopping you from accessing it, and you should. To get a foot in the door of today's organisations, you first need to be on the inside. The next two chapters will show you strategies for finding your way in using your network and your nous.

ACTIONS

- Sign up to receive news alerts and press releases from the FDI agencies of the country / countries you're interested in. Alternatively, subscribe to the website's RSS feed.
- Subscribe to online versions of inflight magazines for the

national and low-cost airlines carriers of the country / countries you're interested in.

- Subscribe to newsletters specialising in the sector/s in which you seek to work in the countries you're interested in e.g. for Ireland, Silicon Republic and its sister publication, Career Republic are invaluable sources of potential job information for those in the tech sector. They also feature inspiring stories of people who've successfully made the move to Ireland for work.

- Keep a running spreadsheet of new FDI announcements. You can follow the example in this chapter or create your own. Highlight those that you're interested in and follow the recruitment procedure stated in the release. Or, better still, pioneer your own.

- Make a note of the names of those mentioned in the press release. Make an independent approach to the named person in the company.

- Keep track of your contacts and follow-up. Persevere.

- For a global FDI overview, download the Ernst & Young attractiveness survey for your region or country of interest.

4. GET INSIDE INTELLIGENCE

BETWEEN JUNE 2014 and the end of August of the same year, I went on a learning spree. I was working on a communications strategy to attract employers from across Europe to publish their vacancies on a pan-European job portal, and it demanded that I put myself inside the mind of an employer.

It wasn't enough to base the strategy on assumptions, or proceed on the basis of anecdote. In the four years since I'd worked in the pan-European recruitment space, I'd spoken to dozens of employers about their recruitment woes. Their anxieties ranged from the lack of quality applications to the vast skills gap between those they needed and those job seekers have. I could recite their litanies like a Shakespearean sonnet.

But, to better understand why employers make the decisions they do, in terms of *how* they recruit and *where* they recruit, I needed to do some research. Rather than just Googling for information that could be fed into a generic and, ultimately, ineffective strategy, I wanted the real scoop. I needed data – facts and figures, quantitative and qualitative. I needed to get on the inside. I needed to 'become' an employer.

Act like a recruiter, think like a recruiter

Empathy in recruitment is an underrated skill. Usually, where it exists, it's the job seeker we tend to empathise with, as we're familiar with his or her plight. We've all been in the position of looking for a job and know the stress that the job search can cause. But, what about the employer? Does the quota stretch to them?

In 2014, Zappos, the online shoe and clothing store, announced that it would stop posting job ads. They didn't just mean on mega job boards like Indeed and Monster.com, but anywhere, including their own website.

The rationale behind the move was that the recruitment process had become depersonalised – in 2013, the company received 31,000 applications and made only one point five percent of hires. This meant they wasted a lot of time screening and rejecting 30,000 unqualified applicants[x] when they could have been doing something else.

Mike Bailen, a senior HR manager at the Zappos Family of Companies, explained it like this: "Instead of posting openings to job boards, we will be marketing openings and headhunting in a very targeted and direct fashion. We will use our existing employees for referrals, run targeted ad campaigns, and aggressively headhunt on various channels... All of our energy and resources will be directed in a purposeful and meaningful way[xi]."

Even the most hardened of job seekers can appreciate the frustration of an employer swamped with unqualified applications. Despite what we may be inclined to think, no employer wants an open vacancy; it hinders growth and goes against their interests.

Unfilled job vacancies cost the British economy £18 billion a year[xii]. Forty-nine per cent of all UK job vacancies remain unfilled after 30 days, and 27% after three months. Vacancies over a month old represent a combined loss of £1.5bn in potential economic output each month[xiii]. And businesses that fail to recruit for positions successfully within the first month of an opening face a 56% chance that their vacancy will remain open for three months or more[xiv]. That's a lot of cash at stake.

If you know what it costs an employer to have an open vacancy, then you know your worth and you can quantify your value. This works out in both yours and the employer's favour and you can appeal to their strategic and their financial head.

To facilitate my recruiter role-play, and acquire a foundation for my task, I started reading reports and studies that were aimed at employers and sought to address their recruitment issues.

I then began attending webinars for employers and recruitment professionals. This gave me a fascinating insight and understanding of everything from recruitment trends to the importance of employer branding in attracting the best candidates.

Here are some things I learned from webinars aimed at HR professionals and recruiters:

- **"Rise to the Top with Employee Referrals,"** a Jobvite and Achievers event that showed me how employers can improve the recruitment experience and entice the best candidates to join their company.

- **"How to Engage Employees: From Passive Candidates to Exceptional Employees,"** Jobvite and BambooHR. As the title suggests, this webinar gave me the inside story on how companies recruit through employee referrals and why it makes sense for them to do so.

- **"2014 Talent Shortage Trends: Understanding the Challenges,"** a ManpowerGroup webinar. An engaging and informative overview of global skills shortages presented by the Vice President of Recruiting Strategy of ManpowerGroup North America.

- **"How to Recruit Healthcare Talent with Social Media,"** run by Work4 [xv] , an agency that advises corporates on talent acquisition through social media. With healthcare being a strong growth sector, I learnt how companies are using new methods to recruit candidates, in this case, social media.

- **"Recipe for Recruiting Success: Great Reviews + Great Career Sites = Happy Hires,"** a joint Jobvite and Glassdoor event. Employers care what you think about them just as much as you care what they think about you. This webinar focussed on why branding is key and how it can be used to attract the best talent.

This kind of research, and the information I gleaned from it, is what I call "Inside Intelligence." The information clearly isn't meant for you as a job seeker, and that's what makes it interesting.

By accessing it, you get a whole new perspective on the

recruitment process, which you can use to your advantage. This inside knowledge and newfound empathy should shine in the approach you craft and the application you write. It could be the difference between the rejection pile and the express lane to a new job.

As a sidebar, by taking some of these webinars, I earned credits that I could use towards gaining a professional qualification. Check to see if the Human Resources Certification Institute, the global training organisation for human resources professionals, accredits the course you take. If it does, you could be onto a winner.

Information is king

So by going the extra mile and thinking like a recruiter, you have nothing to lose and everything to gain, including a potential qualification.

Be in no doubt: information is king. The 360° job seeker knows that "the most successful professionals are those who arm themselves with data,[xvi]" but, they also know to look in unorthodox places to equip themselves with the best tools.

This is where big data comes in, that massive tangle of computational data that the web thrives on, and corporations exploit to their advantage.

Thankfully, it's someone else's job to make sense of this jumble and transform it into manageable information that you can use.

But, first, let's be clear about what big data is and why it should matter to you.

What's big data and what can it do for me?

Although the term, 'big data' has become somewhat trendy both inside and outside tech circles, it's worth reminding ourselves what it actually means:

> big data
>
> *noun*
>
> COMPUTING
>
> 1. extremely large data sets that may be analysed computationally to reveal **patterns, trends, and associations, especially relating to human behaviour and interactions.**
> 2. "much IT investment is going towards managing and maintaining big data"
>
> *My emphasis. Source: Wikipedia*

It's those "patterns, trends, and associations" that are useful for career strategists in helping to formulate strategies for today's labour market, as well as plans for the medium and long-term future.

The application of big data is essential for informed decision-making. Big data can help you find out:

- Where the jobs are, by country, region and city
- What sectors are growing
- What skills are in demand, and where

- Salary information
- What the labour market conditions are
- The cost of living
- Jobs and skills of the future

To illustrate this, here's some interesting data from Ernst & Young's annual European attractiveness survey 2014[xvii], which analyses FDI data and surveys investors about the region's prospects:

- For a majority of our respondents, R&D will be the driving force in Europe's future FDI attractiveness.
- The ICT sector is seen as a key driver of growth in Europe in coming years.
- 25% of our respondents see the pharmaceutical and biotechnology industry as the major driver of European growth in coming years.
- According to one in five investors (+5% compared with last year), the automotive and transport industry will boost Europe's future growth.
- The sheen of the European cleantech sector has faded slightly, with 21% of respondents' votes this year, putting it in 4th position.
- Boosting labor mobility and skills development will be one of the major drivers of Europe's future attractiveness to investors.

These findings about growth sectors in Europe are supported by other studies. That's what big data does; it identifies trends, makes intelligent predictions and invites you to act on them.

And the big data industry, itself, is growing. A recent CNBC article highlighted the scale of investment being ploughed into the sector, signalling a boom in this fledgling industry.

It quoted a survey by a global recruitment firm which found that the most sought-after employees were those with the skills to mine the data mass that the digital revolution had created. However, "There could be a shortage of between 140,000 and 190,000 of these workers by 2018, as industries well beyond tech look for workers who can help them improve their companies by utilising information gleaned from big data.[xviii]"

It's not only companies that should be utilising big data to improve their operations. Smart, strategic job seekers should, too. In the recruitment marketplace, every individual is their own brand and you can better your performance with data.

On another note, in reading this story, the 360° thinker would have immediately recognised that the whole article was a fancifully dressed job lead masquerading as a news story.

See how integrated the 360° method is? I love it when a plan comes together!

Where can I get it?

Those dreaded job boards I berated earlier? Well, not so fast. I did say that they have their uses and this is where they come into play for the 360° job seeker.

Recruitment agencies and job boards charge employers thousands for services ranging from a simple job ad to executive candidate sourcing. They need to justify their services, and diversify their businesses, by showing that their jobs are worth the expense because they solve employers' problems rather than add to them. They hold a mirror up to their clients and magnify the scale. As holders of huge databases of both job seekers and employers, they are in a unique position to take the temperature of the labour market at any given time. Therefore, they produce data.

Most of the major job boards and recruitment agencies have research arms. Familiarise yourself with their work and the areas they specialise in and sign up to receive the latest reports.

Remember, your typical job board / recruitment agency has two main clients: you, the candidate and the employer. As a job seeker, many of them provide you with tips and advice on securing a job through blogs, newsletters and videos on, for example, drafting the perfect cover letter or preparing for an interview.

But, if you register as an employer, you will get a totally different service that will take you behind the scenes of the recruitment process:

- Webinars
- Access to recruiter-only websites and blogs
- Reports and studies
- Employer and recruiter newsletters

To get you started in your new role as candidate-seeking employer, here are some of the most useful resources.

Your essential inside information toolkit

Your essential toolkit for your 360° job search strategy must contain the following. These resources, primarily aimed at employers, are data which is why you would do well to find out what they know so you can give them what they need.

Intelligence	Why?	When
The Manpower Skills Survey	Internationally respected survey that identifies global talent / skills shortages and their impact.	Annually, June
Manpower Employment Outlook Survey	Each quarter, the Manpower Employment Outlook Survey measures hiring confidence among approximately 66,000 employers in 42 countries and territories.	Quarterly
LinkedIn Global Recruiting Trends Report	LinkedIn's annual insights on sourcing, talent brand, and future recruiting trends.	Annually, October

Jobvite Social Recruiting Survey	Find out which social networks are most used by recruiters and how they use social media to find, engage, and nurture candidates. Additionally, see Adecco's Global Social Recruiting Strategy.	Annually

ACTIONS

- Gather the elements of your Inside Intelligence toolkit. Download from appropriate websites. Subscribe to the research or 'insights' arm of the big recruitment agencies to receive key reports when they're published.
- Take at least two webinars aimed at employers and recruiters a month.
- Register with the Human Capital Institute to find out about the latest HR webinars and watch past events, and learn everything from talent acquisition strategy to strategic workforce planning.
- On LinkedIn, follow these Influencers for the latest HR and recruitment insights:
  - o Lou Adler
  - o Alistair Cox
  - o Stacy Zapar
- Follow the company pages of the big recruitment agencies to be notified when they publish new reports and studies.

- Subscribe to these recruitment industry blogs:
  - LinkedIn Talent Solutions
  - Jobvite Recruiting Trends Blog
  - The Ladders Hiring Advice
  - ManpowerGroup Research & Insights
  - ManpowerGroup Right Management
  - Undercover Recruiter
  - ERE.net
  - Glassdoor for Employers
  - Recruitment Buzz
  - Employer Brand News
  - Work4
  - Jobcast
  - Recruiter Today (Recruiter.com)
  - ERE.net
  - Blogging4jobs.com
- Read some Jobvite eBooks for recruiters
- Check in regularly with the big industry associations for your sector. Download reports, go to events, speak to people in the organisation and make yourself known. Do the same with Chambers of Commerce.
- Think like an employer and read like an economist. Pick up Peter Cappelli's *Why Good People Can't Get Jobs: The Skills Gap and What Companies Can Do About It* and Enrico Moretti's *The New Geography of Jobs.* Both give a brilliant overview of the global labour market and, in Cappelli's case, present a compelling counter-narrative to

the prevailing talk of the skills gap while offering alternative solutions.

5. BE PASSIVE AGGRESSIVE

A COUPLE OF years into starting my own business and going it alone, I was feeling overwhelmed. I was going all out to deliver a quality service to existing clients while actively searching for new ones. At the same time, I was doing my best to keep on top of the mountain of paperwork that comes with being a small business owner. After sixteen months of walking this tightrope, and at the brink of exhaustion, I finally accepted that I could no longer do it all by myself. So I set about the process of looking for help.

Rather than placing an ad on an online job board, and be bombarded with a torrent of applications I had no time to process, I chose to send a short email to a close group of friends. The hope was that they would circulate it within their circles or, preferably, make recommendations.

Within days, I'd received some responses. One, in particular, stood out from the rest. It was an email from a woman I didn't know who said that they'd been forwarded my message by their aunt who thought they'd be a good fit for the role I was seeking to fill. She was a recent graduate looking to gain some experience and her eagerness and willingness to learn shone through.

Thanks to Natalie, a former colleague, my assistant, Nandi, was my first company hire. I interviewed and recruited her in the space of three weeks and she soon got to work relieving the pressure.

This kind of relationship-based recruitment isn't uncommon. As I mentioned in the opening chapter, the company I used to work for routinely recruits in this way, as do many others. I know this because recruiters often contact me who say they heard about me through a referral.

And it's not just SMEs who handle their hiring this way. Major multinationals are increasingly turning to staff recommendations to source and hire new staff. Surveys have shown that over 93% of the top performers in their field do not find their job from a job posting; instead, they're referred by someone they know, such as a friend or networking contact[xix]. And only 18% of expat professionals say they found their job through an advert[xx].

If you're not being referred for jobs by your contacts, then you're missing out on access to the 80% share of the job market that serious, career professionals do business in.

But, how do you become a member of this secret jobs society?

Thankfully, there are steps you can take to get into in the hidden job market and start making moves. You just have to learn how to be passively aggressive.

What is passive recruiting and how does it work?

Passive recruiting is the name given to the practice of courting potential candidates who are not currently looking for a job.

Recruiters are attracted to this type of candidate because

they're usually at the top of their game, are well respected by their peers and are therefore highly desirable professionals. There's also the exclusivity. Since passive candidates are not actively looking for a job, they're less likely to be interviewing with other companies meaning that a shrewd recruiter has the opportunity to claim a real scalp.

Recruiters categorise candidates in three groups[xxi]:

- **Active candidates**

  An active candidate is actively looking for work. They may be spending their whole time engaging in job seeking activities or they may be casually looking a few times a week. They're not necessarily unemployed, two-thirds of this group are in employment, and could be looking for a new job for a variety of reasons, including professional development or a higher salary. Active candidates make up 25% of the workforce.

- **Passive candidates**

  Passive candidates, by contrast, are those who are not actively looking for work. They may be happy in the current positions and, therefore, not wanting to move. Passive candidates account for 75% of the workforce. This number jumps to over 90% for high-demand positions and for the strongest talent[xxii].

- **On the Cusp**

  Those in this group, a subset of the latter, aren't actively applying for jobs but are preparing to move, gently asking their networks about opportunities.

Recruiters use a number of strategies to reach out to passive candidates including tapping into their networks and going to events, but a key tool in the sourcing and recruiting of this group is the referral.

An employee referral is when a member of staff recommends or refers the name of a potential employee from his or her professional or personal network to his or her company's HR team. And they're increasingly used by organisations.

At Ernst & Young, employee recommendations now account for 45 per cent of nonentry-level placements. The company's goal is 50 per cent and employee referrals get fast-tracked through the system.

Others companies are just as hawkish. Enterprise Rent-A-Car and Deloitte, which gets 49 per cent of its experienced hires from referrals, have begun offering prizes like iPads and large-screen TVs in addition to traditional cash incentives for employees who refer new hires[xxiii].

The upshot of this is that if you get referred, everyone wins – your referrer with their reward, you with a new job and the organisation with a trusted employee who's likely in it for the long haul.

Why recruiters prefer referrals

This table[xxiv] illustrates why employers prefer referrals. Recruiting staff through recommendation is cheaper, faster and more efficient and effective than traditional recruitment methods[xxv] and, as was noted in the previous chapter, empty desk syndrome costs employers a lot of money.

	Traditional Recruiting	Employee Referrals
Recruiting costs	$4,000-$18,000	$1,000 or less
Time to placement	39 to 45 days	29 days or less
Retention after two years	20%	45%
Hire Rate	1 in 10	1 in 3

You can get in an employer's good books by saving them time and money before they even hire you, which they inevitably will if you exploit your 360° credentials. How? The answer lies in your response to the following question.

Are you a Homer or a purple squirrel?

It's not just the terms 'active,' 'passive' and 'on the cusp' that recruiters use to group candidates. Apparently, in the recruitment world, there is other, less flattering terminology, according to this revealing snippet from a *New York Times* article:

> "You're submitting your résumé to a black hole," said John Sullivan, a human resources consultant for large companies who teaches management at San Francisco State University. "You're not going to find top performers at a job fair. Whether it's fair or

not, you need to have employees make referrals for you if you want to find a job." Among corporate recruiters, Mr. Sullivan said, random applicants from Internet job sites are sometimes referred to as "Homers," after the lackadaisical, doughnut-eating Homer Simpson. The most desirable candidates, nicknamed "purple squirrels" because they are so elusive, usually come recommended[xxvi].

360° job seekers are clearly purple squirrels. They wouldn't dream of feeding their CV into a job board black hole. They see trips to job fairs as fact-finding missions not job finding missions, an opportunity to network and gather information. They know that to get ahead in the job market they have to be active about being passive. And being active means being aggressive - passive aggressive.

Get referred: be passive aggressive

Thanks to the marketing expert, Porter Gale we're all familiar with the saying, "Your network is your net worth." The growth and undeniable clout of referrals is proof that this maxim still holds value. So, how do you get noticed by recruiters without putting your boss on red alert? The simplest way, of course, is to get referred. But, if you don't know anyone on the inside, here's how to make yourself known on the outside so opportunities come to you.

You don't need to advertise the fact that you're looking for a job, but you can still get seen by those with hiring power. Become an expert in your field and share your expertise. Publish, comment, post and blog so that you can connect with your peers and build a community around your ideas. Showcase your knowledge on your own website. Apply the entrepreneurial model to your career [xxvii]. Develop a competitive advantage. Pursue breakout opportunities. Brand yourself.

Follow this five-step programme to passive recruitment success:

1. **Amplify** your achievements to a select audience by engaging in thought leadership, conference speaking, article writing, video blogging etc. Use channels and platforms that you know recruiters in your field engage with. Enumerate and communicate your accomplishments.

2. **Capitalise** on your experience, knowledge and skills. Research potential employers and talk to people inside the organisation to work out how and where you could fit in, culturally and professionally. Then, when you get an in with a recruiter, show how you can solve an organisational problem.

3. **Quantify**. Value yourself, your skills, your experience and what you bring to the table in numerical terms. Quantify everything – past, present and future. Commercialise that value by studying the market, benchmarking your

achievements and finding your niche so that recruiters can find you.

4.   **Specialise** in your field by reading, researching, learning and generating big new ideas. Invest in training and self-development. If you're employed, make the most of your current job by taking as many opportunities to develop as possible.

5.   **Diversify** your network by going out to industry and non-industry events, being on the scene and prospecting, making it easy for recruiters to find you.

Position yourself well. If you're employed, be good in your current job. Make yourself indispensable. Actively solicit recommendations and testimonials. By being a star employee, you will put yourself in prime poaching position for headhunters.

SMEs versus corporates

Everyone wants to work for Google. Whether you're a data scientist, an engineer or a PR executive, it seems working for the search giant is the most desired goal of job seekers.

But the chances of securing a job with one of the world's largest tech giants are about as slim as my chances of winning the lottery. You'd be much better off aspiring to a position within a start-up that could be the next Google and planning your ascent through the ranks than striving for Google itself.

The fact is that 99% of businesses in Europe are small and

medium enterprises. SMEs are responsible for employing millions of people and the opportunities they provide for career development are many. Greater job responsibility, earlier career progression and a higher profile within the business are just a few of the reasons why working at a small company could be for you.

Given that the average corporate job attracts 250 applications – the global accounting firm, Deloitte receives more than 400,000 CVs a year[xxviii] – you'd be wise to focus your efforts on the vast majority of employers who get far fewer applications, but are just as in need of workers as the multinationals.

Scour your network for contacts working in SMEs, particularly those in growth sectors, and ask them to refer you. Not only will you be in with a greater chance, but when you do get on the inside you'll probably be more appreciated, too.

ACTIONS

- Mine your personal and professional contacts. Make it known to your contacts and confidantes that you're looking for work.
- Make a list of those who work in companies that you'd like to work for.
- Ask them if their organisation has an employee referral scheme. If they don't know, ask them to enquire or find out for yourself.
- If there is a scheme, ask them to put your name forward to the relevant person or team in their organisation.

- Be prepared for the conversation that may follow by tapping your contact for inside information about the organisation that could give you a head start.

- Don't forget to do your own research on the company. Familiarise yourself with the organisation's values, culture and accomplishments. Develop a case for how you could help the company achieve its organisational objectives.

- Make your CV and application package mobile-friendly. Save PDF versions of your resume and work samples on Google Drive or Dropbox. Be ready to apply whenever and wherever employers are recruiting.

- Showcase your expertise. Be active online and get socially engaged.

- Get recommended. Actively solicit testimonials from your colleagues, bosses and clients on LinkedIn and other platforms.

- Meet recruiters on their own turf. Go to events for recruiters as opposed to recruitment events. Go where they go and learn what they learn so that you can approach them on the same level (see previous chapter, Get Inside Intelligence).

- Go to events across all sectors. As a communications consultant, I can work in any industry and sector; they all need marketers whether in gas and oil, literature and the arts, tech, legal and charity, etc. Even if you're profession isn't as adaptable, you can still learn from across the knowledge spectrum. Download the Eventbrite app and search for events by type and location to find those that are happening near you. Get out and talk to people. Use Meetup.com to discover informal gatherings and try going to those outside your comfort zone.

- Check out LinkedIn's Talent Blog for the latest articles on passive recruiting.

6. GET MOVING

IN 2014, AS the recession in the United States continued to bite yielding an underclass of long-term unemployed, an article appeared in the *Financial Post* about the impact of the downturn on millennials.

Headlined "Young and unwilling to relocate: How Millennials may be holding back the U.S. labour and housing recovery," the story went that due to a combination of "relatively low-paying opportunities, the burden of student loans and an aversion to taking risks,[xxix]" young people are unwilling to move to where the jobs are. As a result of their collective immobility, they are, as a group, stifling the economic recovery.

At the time of the article's publication, I had been a consultant to the European Commission's EURES service for almost four years. During that time, we had seen the number of contacts to the service rapidly increase as the pain of the recession was felt. Because of my work, I knew that young Europeans, apparently unlike young Americans, were ready and willing to move to another country for the chance of a job.

In fact, so willing are young Europeans to pack up and leave their economically depressed homelands that the political climate in the EU has reached fever pitch. Receiving countries to which jobseekers flock - Germany, Austria, the UK and the Netherlands – have seen a swing to the right while those sending countries that jobseekers leave, e.g. Spain, Greece, Croatia and Italy must face the consequences of the loss of their young and brightest.

I was one of the two per cent of Europeans who choose to live and work in another country. In the spring of 2010, I had a serious professional decision to make. I could either wait to lose my job or be proactive and leave it.

I was just eight months into an eighteen-month contract that had taken my career to the next level. I was the communications manager for a regional pilot of the national Change4Life programme, one of only nine in the country. After years of toiling in a series of high stress, mid-level, low appreciation roles, I was finally in a job that I liked, one in which I was respected by my peers and my bosses, too. I enjoyed getting up and going into work in the morning.

The Change4Life programme was a flagship of the New Labour government. Spearheaded by the Department for Health, its aim was to reduce levels of childhood obesity thereby offsetting its many related illnesses and the consequent cost to the NHS. It was a major national campaign with massive central government support.

But when the May 2010 general election ushered in a new era of Conservative-led coalition government, our team of six, specially recruited, fixed-term workers knew that the programme, along with our jobs, were under threat. Austerity was the order of the day and as the new government sought to assert its authority on the deficit, public sector spending was the main focus of their cuts. It wouldn't be long before we'd be given the axe. As rumour became reality, the mood in the office changed from upbeat to downcast.

Amid the gloom, there was what some of my colleagues considered a ray of light. There was one other option open to us as we faced certain redundancy. It was the one of least resistance. I could, like my colleagues, ask to be placed in the redeployment pool and hope to be placed in another job in another area of the council where I would, most likely, be doing a different job on similar pay.

But was that what I really wanted? I hadn't realised it, but my eyes had already been opened to other, far away possibilities.

A continent of opportunities

While most of my colleagues were successfully redeployed and would stay at the council for years to come, I took a job at a communications agency in Brussels. It was a move that would change the course of my career.

My rationale for the move was simple: why restrict myself to one country when I had access to 31? The EU was, after all, a common market - of labour opportunity. But, rather than think of myself as an expat or an economic migrant, as some would categorise me, I like to think of myself as an entrepreneur.

In their book, *The Start-Up of You,* LinkedIn founder, Reid Hoffman and his co-author, Ben Casnocha advocate adopting an entrepreneurial approach to careers. They argue that in today's constantly evolving labour market, everyone should think of themselves as an entrepreneur at the helm of at least one living, growing start-up venture: their career.

In the chapter "Develop a Competitive Advantage," Reid and Hoffman write: "Some American basketball players not good enough to play in the NBA play successfully in Europe – their skills don't change, but the market does. Picking a market niche where you're better than the competition is key to entrepreneurial strategy."

It's not that I wasn't good enough "to play" in the UK; I just decided not to. By moving to Brussels, I had placed myself in a market in which I had the competitive advantage of being a native English speaker in a city that's home to European and international institutions like the European Commission and Nato.

When I arrived in Belgium in August 2010, I knew no one and had only been to the country twice, briefly, and one of those times was to interview for the job I ultimately got. Now, I was living and working in the capital of Europe with no immediate plans to return home.

And I wasn't alone. In Brussels, I met many others like me, from Britain to Bulgaria, Sweden to Spain, who had taken advantage of the freedom of movement, decamped and moved abroad for work. For us, it was worth the intelligent risk and it could be for you, too.

Why move?

Why not? These days, relocation is relatively easy. Thanks to the proliferation of low-cost airlines and cheap intercontinental train travel, hopping on a plane is like jumping on a bus. Time, money and visa restrictions are no longer the impediments they once were.

A true story: I found it much quicker and less stressful to commute between London and Brussels, which I did for a year, than to commute between Enfield in north London and Teddington in the southwest, a two-and-a-half hour journey each way.

There are now over 200 million people across the globe living and working abroad. The percentage of people who are willing to relocate for work has risen, more than doubling from 16% to 35% in the last five years.

And it's not just those in topflight careers who are going global. Only 17% of people working abroad in 2014 held a professional qualification over and above a first degree[xxx].

Companies, like opportunities, are multinational meaning that finding a job is no longer restricted to the area where you grew up, went to university or live. And employers value international experience according to surveys of both recruiters and expat employees, a quarter of whom believe that international work experience improved career prospects.

The benefits of working abroad include:

- Gaining new skills and experience
- Broadening your network
- Learning a new language
- Immersing yourself in a new culture

Globalisation and technology have made the options for finding work almost as many as there are countries in the world. But, finding a job in another country could also be as simple as paying a visit to your local job centre.

Politics and practicalities

This is why you've never heard of EURES: because your government doesn't want you to hear about it. Although every EU Member State is signed up to the service and is duty-bound to contribute vacancies to the jobs database, the national political climate rather than commitment to the principle of free movement dictates the level of engagement.

In July 2014, the British prime minister, David Cameron wrote an article in *The Daily Telegraph* ahead of a keynote speech in which he promised to cut the number of British jobs advertised on the EURES portal. The speech was, in part, in response to the rising popularity of UKIP, a fiercely anti-Europe party whose raison d'être is to pull Britain out of the EU and drastically cut immigration.

Cameron's speech was headline news in the print and broadcast media. On that night's *Sky News* newspaper review, the *Daily Mail's* associate editor, Andrew Pierce and his counterpart from *The Mirror,* Kevin Maguire went head-to-head in their usual pugilistic style as they discussed the morning's headlines.

As Pierce derided the European Commission and EURES, in particular, for contributing to the flood of migrants stealing British jobs, Maguire sprung to the service's defence in unusual fashion. "Who's ever even heard of EURES?" he said. "Who do you know who's ever got a job through EURES?"

The problem isn't that EURES, a network of 32 public employment services, hasn't found anyone any jobs. The problem is the opposite: since its formation more than twenty years ago, it has helped place thousands of Europeans in jobs in other EU countries. In some ways, the service is a victim of its own success.

What is EURES?

EURES, the European Employment Service, was formed in 1994 as a network of national public employment services, or job centres. Its remit was to provide a transparent information service to EU citizens wanting to take advantage of the right to free movement, which allows them to live and work in any EU country. In light of the economic crisis that has caused unprecedented continental unemployment and movement of labour, its purpose has changed. It now seeks to be a matching tool, which, in plain English, means that its mission is to actively place you as a European citizen in a job that matches your skills, wherever in the EU that job is. Think of EURES as ERASMUS for workers. If you want to get a job in your local area, you go to your high-street recruitment agency. If you want to find a job in another EU country, you go to EURES. That's how it should work in theory, anyway.

EURES' main shop front is its website. The portal at eures.europa.eu has over a million jobs and contains a wealth of information on living and working conditions in each Member

State. It also has contact details for the 900+ EURES Advisers who are the human face of the service.

The website suffers from the same problem as other online mega job boards in that it can be difficult to actually find a job on it, but this is to misunderstand its value, which can be found in what it does rather than what it claims to do.

What can EURES do for you?

- It can tap into the power of its extensive pan-European network.
- It can show you how well your qualifications, skills and experience travel.
- You can speak to a real-life person who speaks your language, a trained adviser with up-to-date information on the EU labour market.
- It can help you choose your relocation destination wisely.
- It can help you with the nitty-gritty of moving abroad, like social security, pensions, family relocation, and the like.
- It can give you advice, information and support through a range of services and platforms including physical and online events.

Notice I didn't mention that it could help you find a job. It can also do that, but the 360° job seeker knows that the only way to find a job is to either find one herself using all the resources at her disposal, or create one.

Don't be like the 157 people who've spent the last year on a LinkedIn forum complaining about EURES not finding them a job when they would have been better off employing the 360° strategy and finding one for themselves.

Exploding EURES myths

- Don't fall into the trap of believing that because the service is free it's worthless. Free just means that someone else is paying for it and that someone isn't you.
- Don't let the stigma of EURES being part of the public employment service put you off. The job centre might suck but some parts suck less than others.
- Just because you haven't heard of it doesn't mean it doesn't exist. Much of the time, our hands were tied and the political always trumps the practical.

While some of the criticisms of EURES may be valid, you have nothing to lose by using the service. In fact, there's potentially much to gain. Its usefulness is its breadth of resources (see next table). My only caveat is that EURES is just one tool of many in your job search arsenal. 360° thinkers should never rely solely on one strategy.

Using EURES to your advantage

What do you need?	How EURES can help
I need information about living and working in another EU country, including up-to-date labour market information and living and working conditions.	**EURES portal** The first port of call for all information, advice and recruitment services for those wanting to live and work in another EU country. Research national labour markets, download publications, get in contact with any one of the 900+ EURES Advisers and search for jobs, if you must.
I want to meet with employers actively looking to recruit from abroad and get advice on living and working in another EU country.	**European Job Days** European Job Days (EJDs) are EURES' flagship public event. The job fairs take place twice a year, in spring and autumn, when each member of the EURES network holds a recruitment event under the EJD banner. In 2012, the Commission introduced European Online Job Days (EOJDs). At an EOJD, recruiters interview job seekers online, wherever they are in Europe, and visitors can speak to EURES Advisers and other EU recruitment experts. Increasingly, EJDs are moving from being general to niche events. For

	example, there are EOJDs for engineers wanting to work in Portugal, for medical specialists looking to work in the Netherlands and customer service staff with EU language skills willing to relocate to Ireland. Visit the EJD website for a list of forthcoming events.
I need to speak to someone in the relocation country of my choice about my European job search.	**EURES Chats** Weekly online chats with EURES Advisers from across the EU answering questions about moving to their country.
I want to read news and features on real people who've moved abroad, as well as tips and advice for successfully living and working in another EU country.	**EURES on social media** Corporate EURES can be found on all the major social networks. • Facebook • LinkedIn • Twitter • Google+ • YouTube Many individual network members have their own, national social media channels, too, which can be found through the EURES website.

I want to look for jobs in any EU country.	**EURES app** Again, if you must search for jobs on a mega online job board, then you might as well download the EURES app and look for employers with jobs who are open to recruiting from abroad.

Living in one country, working in another

You don't have to move to take advantage of the international labour market. If you live close enough to another country in which there are more or better employment opportunities in your line of work, then you could join the thousands of workers who cross-border commute everyday.

It's not uncommon to live in Belgium and work in France or the Netherlands, or reside in France but have your office in Switzerland. The commute between the Slovakian and the Austrian capitals is less than an hour by car.

EURES has over 20 cross-border partnerships, spread geographically throughout Europe involving more than 13 countries. If you're looking to explore your cross-border options, you could start by getting in touch with them.

Look East!

That LinkedIn forum that I spoke about before, the one with 157 comments and 87 likes? There was one commenter who was able to take a step back and bring much-needed reflection to the febrile discussion.

Javier Alonso, a "Specialist in Export | Project Management | International Marketing | Market Research | Trade Financing | Market Entry," was working in the Czech Republic having found a job there through EURES in his native Spain. It wasn't easy and there were many stops and starts, but Javier was now settled in a new job in a new country, thanks to perseverance and an open mind.

I won't reproduce what he said, but you can read his measured contribution to the debate on the EURES, European Employment Services group page, a 360° thinker if ever there was one.

ACTIONS

- Register on the EURES website at eures.europa.eu.
- Read the latest labour market information for the country / countries you want to work in. Check back as the data changes regularly.
- Download living and working brochures for the country / countries you're interested in.
- Contact your local EURES Adviser for a chat about which jobs are in demand now, and where, and how your qualifications and skills translate.
- Search the library of publications for practical guides on moving abroad.

- Download a copy of the EUROFOUND yearbook: Living and Working in Europe

7. GET HIRED!

NOW THAT YOU'VE learnt how to read with your eyes wide open, listen with your ears tuned into the right frequency and consume a range of media more intelligently; now that you know how and where to access big data in all its various forms and analyse it until it becomes accessible so that you can use it to make informed decisions; now that you can tap into the wealth of resources freely available and put yourself inside the mind of an employer; now that you can tap into your existing network for potential job leads, or start building a new one; now that you can think of the world of work in its broadest sense and are no longer restricted by geography or a parochial mentality; now that you know that possibilities and opportunities do exist in abundance and are just waiting for you to proactively go out and seize them; now that you know all this and much more, all that's left is for you to put your newly gained knowledge into practice and act upon it. In other words, start making it work for you so that it yields results.

Remember what we said at the beginning of this journey: without a strategy, you will be lost in the black hole that is today's job search with everyone else. More worryingly, you will feel lost in yourself, frustrated and demotivated, when by simply adjusting your thinking and implementing a few key strategies you could get to where you want to be fast. A strategy is therefore essential in order to plot your route to the job you want. Moreover, the lessons learnt once you get it can and should be used throughout your professional life.

So how do you transform these ideas into a workable, actionable strategy? How do you become more strategic about your hustle?

Pulling it all together: building your strategy

Start with the template available to download from the strategic-hustle.com website. It lays out, in an easy-to-use format, the different elements of the job search that were detailed earlier in the book and that are necessary to cover all bases of the strategic 360 degree approach.

Begin by defining your ultimate objective. What do you want to achieve as a result of this strategy? Where do you want to be in three or six months' time? An example answer to this question formed in an objective might be: "To get a job in Ireland, preferably in Dublin or Cork, in the tech sector within six months."

Then, break down the steps you need to take to reach this goal. This could include signing up to receive FDI alerts from IDA Ireland, creating a Google Alert for Irish tech and business news, signing up to the Silicon Republic newsletter, mining the EURES website for the latest labour market information on Ireland, upgrading to LinkedIn Premium and contacting key people not in your network, registering on Make IT in Ireland, and so on.

Next, having drafted an objective and identified what you need to do to achieve this goal, build your strategy by setting out the tools and channels you'll use to achieve this in a table, as below, being as specific as possible:

360° Element	Objective / Purpose	Tools / Channels
Read, watch, listen	To source potential job leads; to source and make contacts for pursuing those leads.	• Newspapers, magazines and newsmagazines, general and sector-specific. • Television news and business programmes. • Radio news and business programmes.
FDI leads	To source potential job leads; to learn about growth sectors and industries.	• National FDI agencies. • Regional FDI bodies. • Local Enterprise Partnerships. • International FDI information / news sources.
Inside Intelligence	To upgrade skills and expand knowledge of the workings and current trends in	• Attend webinars. • Subscribe to newsletters. • Blogs. • Publications, studies

	recruitment. To understand the mind of a recruiter.	and reports.
Be Passive Aggressive	To zero-in on jobs within specific organisations; to tap into the huge unadvertised job market through referrals, headhunting and relationship-based recruitment.	• Scour contacts. Map which contacts can help in which areas. • Make full use of LinkedIn including its blogs for jobseekers and employers.
Get Moving	To make informed decisions about potential moves abroad in terms of the current labour market and living and working conditions.	• EURES Living and Working information (EU). • EURES labour market information (EU). • Private sector reports and information (International).

Implementing your strategy: your daily action plan

Now that you have your overarching strategy, and you've defined where you want to go, you need to draw up a daily action plan to make sure you get there without getting lost.

This plan, which is based on the strategy, is a practical document that sets out the various steps you will take on a daily, weekly and monthly basis to advance your prospects of finding a quality job as quickly as possible. It should be comprehensive enough to cover all the elements but flexible enough to allow you to modify it as and when necessary.

Depending on your circumstances, below is an example of what your daily schedule might look like if you were implementing this action plan:

Time	Action
6 am	Wake up. Work out. Mentally prepare for the day ahead.
6.30 am	Listen to the morning news programme on the radio. Watch breakfast news on the TV paying particular attention to the business news segments. Jot down any potential job leads plus the names of relevant interviewees.
9 am	Read the quality press online or in print. Save, clip (using Evernote or Pocket) or print any stories with leads. Highlight relevant information including names, job titles and key elements of the story that can be used in the email you'll write as an initial contact e.g. type and number of jobs, location/s, reasons for these openings i.e. the problem that these new posts aim to solve.

10 am	Check your email for newsletter and press release subscriptions. Check out the websites of relevant agencies, news media, blogs etc.
11 am	LinkedIn: Use this time to research and to connect with your existing network and expand your network. Search those mentioned in the job leads gained from the sources above.
12 pm	End the active part of your 360° Job Search day. But, while you're going about your usual business, passively be on the lookout for potential leads and learning opportunities. Depending on your schedule, you may actively pursue these other 360° activities below:
4 pm	Read reports, publications, studies on the labour market and current recruitment and labour market trends including growth sectors, skills gaps.
5 pm	Attend Inside Intelligence webinar.
6 pm / 10 pm	Watch / listen to the evening news. Pay particular attention to the newspaper review segment in the late night news.
7 pm	Take a Skillshare / Udemy class.

Of course, you should adapt this action plan to suit your individual circumstances and habits. If you work full-time, or are a late riser, it won't be possible to implement every one of the above elements at the suggested times but you could do one or two elements in the evenings, catch replays and repeats of radio and television shows and webinars online and double-up on the elements on the weekends.

Perhaps, one day you may not have any FDI data to analyse and follow-up. Therefore, you may choose to focus on mining the news more or reaching out to, or expanding, your network.

Repeat this schedule until it becomes second nature to you. The more you put it into practice, the more adept you'll become at spotting opportunities while "off-duty" that you'll subconsciously pick up and connect with. Investing a little time and effort in implementing this action plan is an investment that will reap dividends for years to come.

Tips for staying on track

Even with these recession-proof strategies, searching for work is no easy task. It's time-consuming, mentally and emotionally draining, and this particular approach requires a complete shift in thinking from the old ways of looking for a job to the new ways of finding one.

With this in mind, here are a few tips to help you stay the course with your strategy and not get discouraged:

- **Make it visual**

  Rather than typing up your strategy as a purely text document and filing it away in the depths of your computer's hard drive, make it a visually attractive publication. By personalising your strategy and transforming it into something that you would want to pick up and refer to, you will feel more inclined to consult it. As well as the hard factual information of data, targets and objectives, think of your strategy as a document for visualising where you see your future professional self, like a vision board. Add images. Make use of Infographics to enliven sterile data. Spread the love by supporting the freelance economy. Hire the services of a designer on Fiverr to layout and design your strategy. Make it beautiful enough to admire but real enough to act on.

- **Tell others about it (but be selective about who you confide in)**

  Obviously, you'll be making the most of your network by tapping them for potential job leads, referrals, informal informational chats, and the like. But, you may also want to tell others in your circle about your new job search strategy. Doing this may help to keep you on track and stop you from wavering when the going gets tough, which it inevitably will. But, be careful about who you confide in. Choose only your most trustworthy friends and colleagues as confidantes and mentors in order to avoid any unnecessary fallout.

- **Join or start a support circle**

  Looking for a job can be a lonely endeavour but you are not alone, nor should you be. Connect with others who are also adopting a strategic approach to job-hunting by joining a Meetup group for likeminded people. And, if there isn't one, consider starting your own group. Register on the www.strategic-hustle.com website and engage with other 360° job seekers virtually. Share ideas, leads and experiences and offer mutual support and inspiration. Or get together with a group of friends in a similar position and meet regularly to offer each other mutual support.

- **Commit to it**

  Be in it for the long haul. Be prepared to commit anything from four to six months putting your strategy into action. This means reading, researching, analysing and reaching out to organisations and individuals on a daily basis for the foreseeable future. Make it a way of life. Commit to reconfiguring your mindset when it comes to the new strategic hustle.

- **Revise it regularly**

  Just because you've written your strategy doesn't mean it's set in stone. In fact, because you've invested time and effort thinking about it, drafting it, crafting it and refining it, it makes sense to track your progress to ensure that it's worth continuing in the same vein or deciding whether you need to tweak, change or drop a few elements in favour of others. The following section explains how to monitor and evaluate the progress of your strategy to ensure it's delivering the results you desire in a reasonable amount of time.

Monitoring and evaluation

The process of monitoring and evaluating may, at first, seem a little dull, especially when compared to the cut-and-thrust of implementation, like networking. But, done correctly, it should be fun, providing a much-needed boost to your energies. By charting your progress and seeing how far you've come in a quantifiable way, you'll be inspired to continue implementing your plan with even more vigour.

Even if you haven't progressed as much as you'd like, monitoring and evaluation will help you figure out why, and give you insights into plotting a way forward. Without this information, you wouldn't know which elements are working and, therefore, to intensify, and which elements are not and where to make changes.

To make your monitoring and evaluation more impactful and efficient, quantify everything. Ensure your targets are SMART – Specific, Measurable, Achievable, Realistic, Time-bound - and don' be afraid to take action based on the evidence you find, whether minor or drastic.

Element	Target	Actual	Action after 1, 3 and 6 months
Read, watch, listen	5 job leads a week 5 contacts approached / made	No. of job leads this week No. of contacts approached	Modify, Increase / Decrease, Abandon
FDI leads	3 FDI leads a week 3 contacts approached / made	No. of FDI leads this week No. of contacts approached	
Inside Intelligence	2 webinars a month 2-4 publications a month	No. of courses taken this week / this month No. of reports, studies, publications, blog posts digested this week / month	
Be Passive Aggressive	2 contacts a week 2 contacts a week	No. of existing contacts re-contacted No. of new contacts made	
Get Moving	TBD TBD TBD	No. of countries targeted (LMI information) No. of visits to EURES or other LMI websites No. of contacts with EURES Adviser/s	

Get hired!

So, there you have it. You're now all set to take charge of your career and get guerrilla about your job search in a strategic way. Now, get set, apply yourself and get hired.

And when you do get hired having used the strategies in this book, please don't keep it to yourself. Celebrate your success by emailing us at info@strategic-hustle.com and allow us to cheer along with you.

Good luck!

APPENDIX: RESOURCES

Your job search toolkit

Apps: Chrome extensions	
Most of these apps are free for the basic service.	
Rapportive	Rapportive shows you everything about your contacts right inside your inbox. Get LinkedIn profiles right inside your Gmail. Get to know your contacts, grow your network and establish your rapport. Free add-on for Firefox and Chrome.
Yesware	Yesware is a great app that lets you track when emails get opened, save email templates, set reminders to follow up, and sync with Salesforce and other CRMs. Also available as a mobile app.
Insightly	Customer Relationship Management (CRM) tool for keeping track of contacts, networking and follow-up actions.

Right Inbox	Allows users to schedule emails to be sent at a later time or date. Can also set email reminders and schedule recurring emails.
Evernote	Take notes, track tasks, and save things you find online. Automatically syncs everything between your phone and computer. Also available as a mobile app.
Apps: Mobile	
LinkedIn	Needs no introduction. Suffice to say, the apps helps you make and nurture connections while on the move.
Newsle	Not an app, but a great LinkedIn add-on that finds blogs and articles that mention you or anyone in your network – colleagues, bosses, friends, or industry thought leaders – and notifies you seconds after they're published.
Google Docs / Google Drive	Great for applying for jobs when on the move through a smartphone. Create and edit web-based documents, spreadsheets, and presentations. Store documents online and access them from any computer.

Dropbox	A storage and file-sharing alternative to Google Drive. Also available as a Chrome extension.
TuneIn Radio	TuneIn enables people to discover, follow and listen to what's most important to them — from sports, to news, to music, to talk. TuneIn provides listeners access to over 100,000 real radio stations and more than four million podcasts streaming from every continent.
Skype	Video calls, voice calls, group calls, screen sharing, instant messaging and file sharing for free. Upgrade your service and get a local Skype number and call forwarding so that you're reachable while on the move wherever you are in the world.
Udemy	A platform or marketplace for online learning with over 300,000 courses in everything from programming to yoga to photography.
Skillshare	Like Udemy, but for creatives.

Useful career-related websites

- Brazen Careerist
- The Muse
- Idealist
- Official LinkedIn blog
- Monster blog

For a comprehensive list, see Forbes Top 100 Websites For Your Career.

CHAPTER TWO: Read Between the Lines

Example One: "A job advert dressed up as a news story"

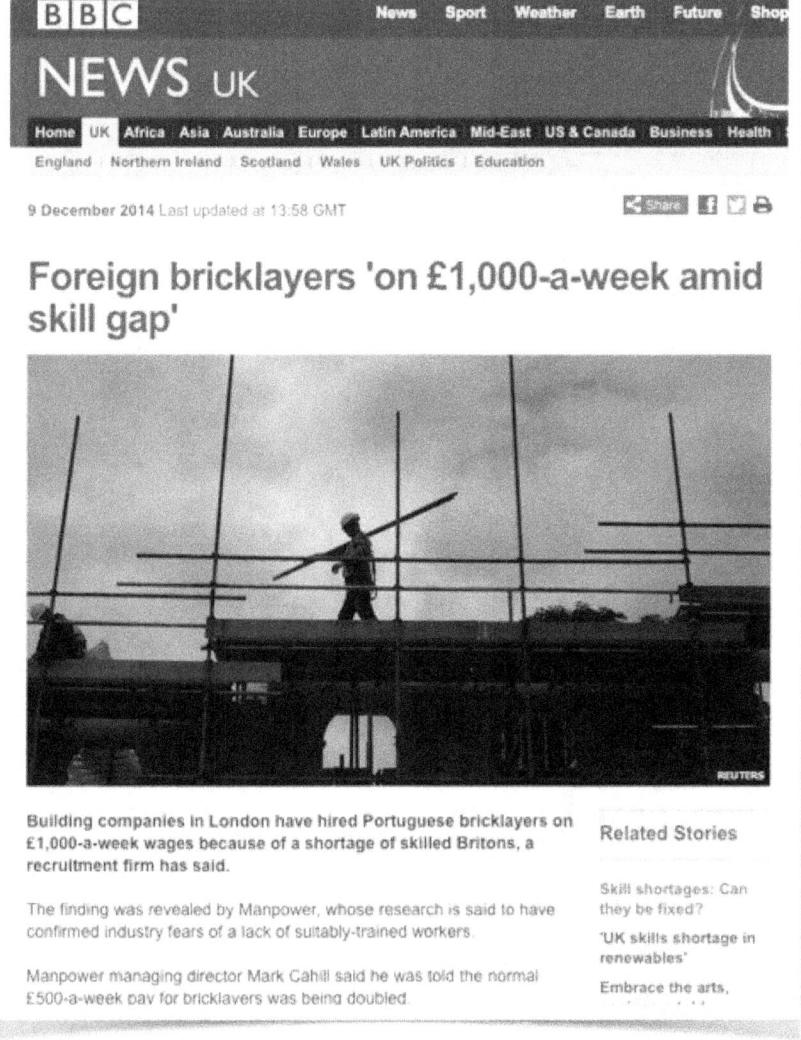

Example Two: "A job advert dressed up as a news story"

Dyson to create 3,000 science and engineering jobs by 2020

By Tanya Powley, Manufacturing Correspondent

Dyson, the bagless vacuum cleaner maker, has unveiled plans to create 3,000 science and engineering jobs in the UK by 2020 as part of the largest expansion in its 20-year history.

The manufacturer plans to invest £250m to expand its Wiltshire-based headquarters and double the size of its research and development centre.

More

ON THIS TOPIC
Car industry says 2014 output will fall

Domestic demand lifts UK manufacturers

UK manufacturers hit by eurozone woes

E-cigarettes bring business to Liverpool

IN UK BUSINESS
Senior City staff expect 21% bigger bonus

Balloniars fails to gag news deal ciles

Desmond explores sale of Daily Express

Qatar makes Tottenham Hotspur its goal

Sign up now

Dyson, which employs about 4,500 across three sites in the UK and Asia, has submitted plans to its local council to create a new technology campus, with R&D laboratories split over four buildings.

The company plans to hire 400 UK engineers this year, on top of the 650 it hired globally in 2013.

The news comes at a time of growing optimism surrounding the UK economy and manufacturing, with figures published on Wednesday showing a sharp fall in unemployment.

Dyson employs 2,000 in the UK, of which half are engineers. The group attracted widespread criticism in 2002 when it decided to outsource production to Malaysia, with the loss of 560 jobs.

Sir James Dyson, the eponymous owner and founder, said the recruitment drive was essential to develop advanced technology. "We hope to create the space for them here in Malmesbury, but with a shortfall of 61,000 engineers every year in the UK, finding them is difficult."

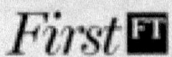

FirstFT is our new essential daily email briefing of the best stories from across the web

The company said it still viewed the UK as a "great place to invent" despite the shortfall of engineers.

Dyson's announcement follows news in December that JCB, the world's third-largest maker of construction equipment, would create 2,500 UK jobs by 2018.

The recent growth comes after a steady decline in manufacturing employment. British manufacturing now stands at 2.4m – 300,000 less than before the financial crisis.

RELATED TOPICS UK manufacturing, United Kingdom, UK employment

CHAPTER THREE: FYI: FDI

Top 25 European Cities Overall for Foreign Direct Investment in 2014

RANK	CITY	COUNTRY
1.	London	UK
2.	Helsinki	Finland
3.	Eindhoven	Netherlands
4.	Cambridge	UK
5.	Dublin	Ireland
6.	Munich	Germany
7.	Barcelona	Spain
8.	Berlin	Germany
9.	Amsterdam	Netherlands
10.	Reading	UK
11.	Edinburgh	UK
12.	Vienna	Austria
13.	Glasgow	UK
14.	Rotterdam	Netherlands
15.	Lyon	France
16.	Paris	France
17.	Grenoble	France
18.	Utrecht	Netherlands
19.	Birmingham	UK
20.	Ghent	Belgium
21.	Liverpool	UK

22.	Lisbon	Portugal
23.	Derby	UK
24.	Cork	Ireland
25.	Galway	Ireland

(Source: fDi magazine)

ACKNOWLEDGMENTS

I would like to thank the following people for their feedback and inspiration:

Becky Blake, Tamara Gausi, Nebojsa Milenkovic, Appiah Kusi Adomako, Natalie Kokayi, Athena Kugblenu, Nandi Nkushi and Saff Mitten.

In addition: Havard Flakne, Patricija Kezele and Daniel Bellon.

EURES Spain, EURES Croatia, EURES Ireland, EURES France, EURES Netherlands, EUREsco and the entire EURES network, in particular, members of the ICWG.

ABOUT THE AUTHOR

Sylvia Arthur was a communications consultant to the European Commission's EURES service for four years (2011-2015). During that time, she travelled across Europe advising government departments and agencies involved in employment and job creation on communicating the benefits of free movement to their citizens. EURES is a network of 32 EU and EEA public employment services charged with promoting intra-EU job mobility to Europe's 500 million citizens. It was thrown into the spotlight in June 2014 when British prime minister, David Cameron pledged to cut by half the number of British vacancies advertised on the pan-European jobs portal, making headline news.

Sylvia is the director of Gordon Square Communications, a corporate communications agency specialising in strategy, internal communications and organisational development.

Connect with her on LinkedIn: be.linkedin.com/in/sylviaarthur or at www.strategic-hustle.com.

REFERENCES

i http://employers.glassdoor.com/statistical-citations/

ii http://www.ibtimes.co.uk/jobs-site-indeed-com-double-european-workforce-substantial-recruitment-drive-1483598

iii http://www.monster.com/about

iv http://mobile.nytimes.com/2013/01/28/business/employers-increasingly-rely-on-internal-referrals-in-hiring.html

v http://www.prweek.com/article/1168031/hill+knowlton-strategies-launches-african-expansion-plan-six-offices

vi http://www.ey.com/GL/en/Issues/Business-environment/european-attractiveness-survey-2014-europe-in-five-years

vii http://www.ft.com/cms/s/0/5a4f687e-e27a-11e3-a829-00144feabdc0.html

viii IDA Ireland

ix http://www.wsj.com/articles/SB10001424127887324576304579072773954985630

x http://www.eremedia.com/ere/what-no-job-postings

xi Ibid

xii http://www.telegraph.co.uk/finance/jobs/11278720/How-empty-desks-cost-the-UK-economy-18bn-a-year.html

xiii http://www.onrec.com/news/news-archive/unfilled-vacancies-costing-the-uk-economy-%C2%A318bn-a-year

xiv Recruitment Buzz, 26 January, 2015

xv http://www.hci.org/lib/how-recruit-healthcare-talent-social-media

xvi http://info.theladders.com/career-advice/big-data-for-better-career

xvii http://www.ey.com/GL/en/Issues/Business-environment/european-attractiveness-survey-2014-europe-in-five-years

xviii http://www.cnbc.com/id/102730230

xix http://www.forbes.com/sites/meghanbiro/2014/08/03/smart-recruiting-strategy-drives-relationships-and-conversation/

xx Global professionals on the move, Fifth edition 2014, Hydrogen Group

xxi http://talent.linkedin.com/blog/index.php/2013/12/recruiting-active-vs-passive-candidates

xxii https://www.surveymonkey.com/results/SM-QF7JWRDV/

xxiii http://www.nytimes.com/2013/01/28/business/employers-increasingly-rely-on-internal-referrals-in-hiring.html?_r=1

xxiv *Rise to the Top with Employee Referrals,* Jobvite webinar, 5 August, 2014

xxv Ibid

xxvi http://www.nytimes.com/2013/01/28/business/employers-increasingly-rely-on-internal-referrals-in-hiring.html?_r=1

xxvii http://www.thestartupofyou.com/

xxviii http://www.nytimes.com/2013/01/28/business/employers-increasingly-rely-on-internal-referrals-in-hiring.html?_r=0

xxix http://business.financialpost.com/news/economy/young-and-unwilling-to-relocate-how-millennials-may-be-holding-back-the-u-s-labour-and-housing-recovery

xxx Global professionals on the move, Fifth edition 2014, Hydrogen Group

www.ingramcontent.com/pod-product-compliance
Lightning Source LLC
Chambersburg PA
CBHW070816180526
45168CB00002B/634